P9-DWK-428

A Gift For:

_____

From:

_____

Shine On, Beautiful Soul!

A Book for Friends

Hallmark

Ellie Claire
gift & paper expressions

...inspired by life

Written by Jennifer Gerelds
Art by Terri Conrad
Interior design by Garborg Design Works | garborgdesign.com

ISBN: 978-1-59530-731-6
BOK2192

Made in China

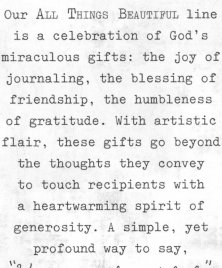

Our ALL THINGS BEAUTIFUL line
is a celebration of God's
miraculous gifts: the joy of
journaling, the blessing of
friendship, the humbleness
of gratitude. With artistic
flair, these gifts go beyond
the thoughts they convey
to touch recipients with
a heartwarming spirit of
generosity. A simple, yet
profound way to say,
"*You are beautiful.*"

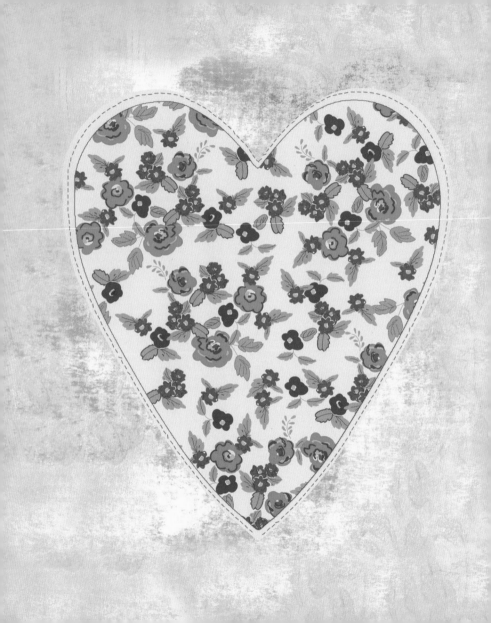

All things bright and beautiful,
All creatures great and small,
All things wise and wonderful,
The Lord God made them all.

CECIL FRANCES ALEXANDER

Introduction

Radiant sunsets. Shimmering rainbows. Towering mountains.
Crashing waves. Throughout the universe, God calls our
attention toward the beauty of what He has made, of who
He is. Life's beautiful surprises beckon us to celebrate.
To wonder. To reflect on a purpose greater than ourselves.

You, dear friend, are one of those miracles.

You may have forgotten or perhaps never have known how
your heart shines like a glowing star against life's darkest
nights, but it does. The God who made you sees it, and so do
your friends. This book was written to remind you of all the
ways you matter to God and the people around you. To paint
a proper perspective of the masterpiece God is making of you.
To encourage you to keep on being the wonderful, cherished,
inspiring person that you are. Never underestimate your
worth. Remember how deeply you are loved. Shine on,
beautiful soul!

Jennifer Gerelds

Do you *see yourself as special* in God's eyes? Or are you weary from wading through hardships, longing for God's favor? God knows you believe in Him, but do you know He believes in you? His heart is filled with desire and determination to bless, help, and promote you. He wants to treat you "special." Are you ready to let Him?

Consider for a moment the *unique beauty and beloved spirit* that you are, created with infinite possibilities. You are His beloved child, unique in every possible way. He wants you to begin to take steps each day to encourage, nurture, and *inspire your beautiful spirit to shine* "as we think in our hearts, so are we" (Proverbs 23:7). You were created by the finest hands and with the deepest, unconditional love of the Creator whose abiding love is always with you. He is for you. He believes in you. *Shine on!*

Terri Conrad

serve

share

smile

with your whole being

Eternity's Dream Child

For he chose us in him before the creation of the world to be holy and blameless in his sight.

EPHESIANS 1:4 NIV

We live in a world of over six billion people. Can you imagine trying to keep track of all those faces, those names, those life stories? The magnitude of it all can be overwhelming. Your own significance comes into question. Can a single life, like a drop of water in the ocean, really matter?

God says you are no ordinary raindrop. You are chosen. Planned. Accounted for...from before time even began! You were in God's mind and heart before a single plant graced the face of the earth. Before the sun even rose to shine. Before the first sound of laughter filled the air.

You were God's smile, the pleasure of His creation. He knew it was good. Master storyteller that He is, he waited patiently for the perfect reveal, the moment your special life should be made known to the world.

Can a single life matter? It certainly does when it is crafted and planned by the God of creation. He made you for this very moment, to be a blessing and beacon of hope to the other lives around you. How will you shine today?

God not only knows us, but He values us highly in spite of all He knows...You and I are the creatures He prizes above the rest of His creation. We are made in His image, and He sacrificed His Son that each one of us might be one with Him.

JOHN FISHER

I knew you before you were formed within your mother's womb; before you were born I sanctified you and appointed you as my spokesman to the world.

JEREMIAH 1:5 TLB

Unforgettable

Can a mother forget the baby at her breast and have no compassion on the child she has borne? Though she may forget, I will not forget you! See, I have engraved you on the palms of my hands.

ISAIAH 49:15–16 NIV

As much as you might wish sometimes, life isn't static. Instead, God makes it a vibrant, dynamic phenomena, pulsating with myriads of activities, thoughts, and people. It can be both exhilarating and tiring to the core. In fact, the more other people's lives infiltrate your own, the more dizzying the effect can be. If you're not careful—and sometimes even when you are—you start to forget things: where you put your keys, that person's name, why you walked into that room in the first place. Suddenly, you start fearing early onset dementia.

Relax, dear friend. You are not deficient (except possibly in sleep). You are merely human, and humans weren't made to multi-task all the responsibilities in the world at once. Good for you, though, you have a daddy who does—your Abba, Father.

He never lets a single moment slip between His fingers without precise direction and purpose. He doesn't forget you either because—well, for one, He's God. But He also keeps a list. Not a Santa Claus list or a record of your sins. It's a list of His children—a list He will never lose, because He has carved each name on the palm of His hand. You are such a treasure that you are a permanent part of who God is. No matter where you go or what you do, your place in God's heart is secure in His hands.

God is a rich and bountiful Father, and He does not forget His children, nor withhold from them anything which it would be to their advantage to receive.

J. K. MACLEAN

I, the LORD,
made you,
and I will not
forget you.

ISAIAH 44:21 NLT

A Different Star

Do everything without grumbling or arguing, so that you may become blameless and pure....Then you will shine among them like stars in the sky as you hold firmly to the word of life.

PHILIPPIANS 2:14–16 NIV

Have you ever wondered what made the wise men notice the star that led them to Jesus? Was it brighter? A different color? Shape? Size? The Bible doesn't say. It only reports that it was different from the rest, it was something the men had been anticipating, and it matched their expectations—all the way to Jesus.

In society today, being recognized as influential and important—in essence, becoming a star—dominates the headlines. Everyone wants to make a difference, to be noticed and celebrated for their brilliant glory. The problem is that we are only human. Vessels made of earth and clay, not stardust. Even celebrity fame falls impotent to bring the lasting value we crave.

But what if that clay pot was filled with light from the inside? Then what was dead and lifeless on its own could achieve the function and brightness desired.

Child of God, you may be a jar of clay, but you have been created to shine out divine glory. Our heavenly Father has filled each believer with His very own presence. His light shines a different, brighter, deeper color than anything people can conjure on their own. You stand apart like the star of Bethlehem, unique and brilliant. Not because you have manufactured greatness, but because God has placed His presence and power in you. So let your light shine. And may the love and power of God within you light the way for others to find Jesus too.

It doesn't take a huge spotlight to draw attention to how great our God is. All it takes is for one committed person to...let his light shine.

GARY SMALLEY AND JOHN TRENT

Those who are wise shall shine like the brightness of the sky above; and those who turn many to righteousness, like the stars forever.

DANIEL 12:3 ESV

Love Songs

The LORD...will rejoice over you with gladness,
He will quiet you with His love,
He will rejoice over you with singing.

ZEPHANIAH 3:17 NKJV

Try riding in your car without turning on music.
Or shopping, eating at restaurants, or exercising at the gym.
It's almost painful to consider because life flows better with
a melody.

The truth is, music has power—an almost inexplicable
ability to connect with our life situations. Even though we didn't
write the song or know the person who did, a lyric or a melody
can match the inner workings of our soul, and make us feel
happy, energized, contemplative, and most of all, known. We
imagine that it was, on some level, written for us—not only to
tell our story about life, love, and identity, but also to invite us to
a deeper spiritual place where words alone can't take us.

But what if you turned on the radio and found out the song playing was specifically written to you—not just any song, but a love song truer than any you had ever heard before? Wouldn't the power of that song be multiplied a thousand times?

Beloved, tune in to your heavenly Father. He is so in love with you, delighted in you, that the God of all creation has written a song just for you. Better still, He is singing it over you at this very moment. *Can you imagine what it sounds like to hear God sing—about you?*

Let the melody of God's pleasure in you drown out the noise of self-contempt and earthly pressures. You have a true connection with Someone more genuine than any other relationship on earth. It's a rhythm of real and lasting love that will leave you singing your own beautiful song right back to Him.

True joy is the heart's harmonious response to the Lord's song of love.

A. W. Tozer

As a bridegroom
rejoices over
his bride,
so will your God
rejoice over you.
Isaiah 62:5 NIV

Fully Known

You have searched me, LORD,
and you know me.

PSALM 139:1 NIV

What makes falling in love so great? At last, you have found the one...the one person who understands you, who knows how you tick and makes you smile, who knows your flaws but loves you anyway. Life seems full of future promise since you won't have to do it alone. But if initial attraction is so much fun, why is marriage so much work? And why do so many marriages end in divorce?

Knowing someone—and being known by them—is not as easy as it may first appear. Your soul is a deep well of thoughts and emotions that change with age and life experience. Keeping in touch with all the inner workings of another person is as difficult as it is keeping tabs on what's going on in your own heart. The complexity can get isolating. It's how even in a crowd—or a marriage—you can feel alone.

But you are never alone. No matter how badly your friends, your boss, your children, or even your spouse may misunderstand you, there is One who knows you, who sees deeply into every secret place in your heart and reads you better than you do yourself.

At first, such deep knowing can seem unnerving. As badly as you want to be known, you're happy to keep the unseemly parts of your psyche hidden. After all, who would still love you if they saw all of you—the good and the bad?

Jesus would. The God who made you, who sacrificed His life to bring you forgiveness, hope, and joy, not only knows all of you, but also loves you more than you can imagine. Find your soul mate in Him. He will never leave you. It's His promise for all of eternity.

To fall in love with God is the greatest of all romances.

AUGUSTINE

LORD, you know my heart. You see me and test my thoughts.

JEREMIAH 12:3 NLT

Race Runner

Those who hope in the LORD will renew their strength.
They will soar on wings like eagles; they will run and not grow weary,
they will walk and not be faint.

ISAIAH 40:31 NIV

Have you ever run or exercised so hard that your legs start to burn? Determined to reach your fitness goal, you press on. But suddenly your limbs seem heavier, awkward, hard to move. Then you realize, you're wiped out. Water and a little breather are required if you want to get back in the game.

Sometimes service for God can feel that way. You start off marriage, the parenting years, maybe a volunteer position with all the energy and enthusiasm in the world. But as you pour yourself out for others, you start to feel the drain. Looking around, you notice not many bother to reciprocate or even appreciate what you're giving. You begin to wonder if it's worth it.

Don't lose sight of the finish line. You are running the race God has given you. Though others may not notice your sacrifice, God does. You are not running in vain, you are running for the prize—Jesus, Himself. As you learn to lean into Him for strength, His living water refreshes your soul. In time, sometimes a long time, you start to see your perseverance pay off. God promises that you will reap a harvest if you just don't give up.

So if your soul is tired, take some time to drink in God's life-giving water. Rest until you catch your breath. But don't walk away from the race. Restore your hope in the Lord and watch Him renew your strength.

By reading of Scripture I am so renewed that all nature seems renewed...The sky seems to be...a cooler blue, the trees a deeper green...and the whole world is charged with the glory of God.

THOMAS MERTON

Let us run with endurance the race that is set before us, looking to Jesus, the founder and perfecter of our faith.

HEBREWS 12:1–2 ESV

God's Home

Do you not know that your body is a temple of the Holy Spirit
within you, whom you have from God? You are not your own,
for you were bought with a price. So glorify God in your body.

       1 Corinthians 6:19–20 ESV

In the Garden of Eden, God came every day for a visit.
When the cool of the day settled, He walked among His
brilliant flowers and trees with Adam and Eve, the most
cherished part of His creation.

What must it have been like, being that close to God? you wonder.
And you wish that sin hadn't wrecked the whole picture.

Yet God is an amazing puzzle maker. Just when it looked
like all of life's beauty was shattered, He began putting the
pieces together in a way no one would have guessed.

God wasn't content to just walk beside His people. In the
Old Testament, we see Him move right into the center of their
camp, living in the tabernacle among them.

However, God wanted to be closer. So Jesus came—God in human form. He became one of us, and paved the way so we could live with Him forever.

But God still wasn't close enough. He wanted in—all in. So He put His own Spirit right inside His children, making them living temples. Though you may sometimes wish your earthly body was built a better way, God says you are just perfect for His presence. Let His Spirit fill you up with the warmth, light, and love that always and forever remains when Christ dwells inside. As His child, you bring the very presence of God everywhere you go.

God knows the rhythm of my spirit and knows my heart's thoughts. He is as close as breathing.

The Spirit of God, who raised Jesus from the dead, lives in you.
ROMANS 8:11 NLT

Lost and Found

*There is joy in the presence of the angels
of God over one sinner who repents.*
LUKE 15:10 NRSV

You didn't mean for it to happen. It seems like one day you were close to Christ, but little by little, your fervor started to fade. Distractions crept into your time with the Lord. Old sins started to resurface. The tyranny of the urgent overtook your prayer time and off you went running to keep life from falling apart.

Then you look up, and feel lost. Where are you? More importantly, where did God go? Have you wandered so far off you can't find your way back? And if you did, what would God say when you got there?

For starters, He'd throw a party. Wrap you in His own robe, put a ring on your finger, and have a feast in your honor. God doesn't take it lightly when you leave Him. He longs for you. Misses you. Searches for ways to reach your soul, and celebrates like crazy once He does. Jesus illustrates the idea through three different stories: the shepherd with ninety-nine sheep who won't rest until the lost one is found; the woman with ten coins who calls all her neighbors over for a party once she finds the one missing coin; and the story of the father whose son left home to squander his inheritance, and returns empty-handed to find his father running down the road to meet him, rejoicing at his return.

Has your heart wandered from home? What are you waiting for? Your Father has been on the lookout for you, and He is waiting for you with open arms. Just turn around and see.

God is the shepherd in search of His lamb... He scales the cliffs and traverses the fields... He cups His hands to His mouth and calls into the canyon. And the name He calls is yours.

MAX LUCADO

He has removed our sins as far from us as the east is from the west.

PSALM 103:12 NLT

27

God's Ambassador

We are ambassadors for Christ,
God making his appeal through us.

2 CORINTHIANS 5:20 ESV

"Just who do you think you are?!" you might have been asked as a kid after saying or doing something impertinent. The reprimand was intended to get you back in line.

As adults, though, that question flows around our thoughts like an unsettling breeze. "Just who *do* I think I am?" Of course, you have your spouse, kids, school, and work that make their demands and fill your time. But they don't answer the question.

Fortunately, God does. He wants you to remember that above all the things you do and say and have and want, you are His precious child. You have your very identity because He made you, loves you, and has a plan for your life. So just who does He say that you are?

You are His ambassador, defined by the dictionary as *a diplomatic official of the highest rank, sent by one sovereign or state to another as its resident representative.* You are of royal blood, sent by the King of kings into this broken world to reconcile people to the God who made and loves them.

It's easy to sag under the world's negativity and frustrations and forget your higher calling. Look up! You are God's official of the highest rank, sent to represent Him to your neighbor, your child's school, the cashier at the grocery store. No moment will ever be mundane again. Your purpose is to love God and lead others to a restored relationship with Him.

Recognizing who we are in Christ and aligning our life with God's purpose for us gives a sense of destiny...It gives form and direction to our life.

JEAN FLEMING

God has given us the privilege
of urging everyone to come into
his favor and be reconciled to him.
2 CORINTHIANS 5:18 TLB

29

together

we can

dream

big dreams

A true friend
inspires you to
believe the best
of yourself, to
keep pursuing
your deepest
dreams.

A True Friend

Then Jonathan made a covenant with David, because he loved him as his own
soul. And Jonathan stripped himself of the robe that was on him and gave it to
David, and his armor, and even his sword and his bow and his belt.

1 Samuel 18:3–4 ESV

The tabloids today are filled with stories of treachery. Just
when a celebrity's life couldn't seem better, a trusted friend
betrays a family secret, or cheats with someone else. It's a
wonder why the not-so-famous people pay good money to
read them.

Maybe it's to add drama to an average life. Or the shock
value of scandal. But maybe it's because it makes us remember
that fame isn't all glory, and good friends are gifts who can't
be bought.

And maybe that's why the friendship between Jonathan and
David is so amazing. Jonathan, son of King Saul, was poised
to be Israel's next king. But when he heard David, a common
Israelite speak before his father, Jonathan was more than

moved. Shockingly, he committed to always be David's friend, even if it meant giving David his throne. Proving his loyalty, he removed his royal armor and gave it to David, a graphic picture of Jonathan's determination to do whatever it took to make David prosper.

Such loyalty hardly computes. Does anyone like that exist in the world today?

The friend who may have given you this book says yes. And you may have been that good friend, giving of yourself to better others. Moreover, Scripture reminds you that you also have a Friend who sticks closer than a brother. Like Jonathan, Jesus gave up His royal robes to cover you in righteousness and call you His forever friend. It is His steadfast love that strengthens you to become a faithful friend to others.

True friends have one soul between them.

There is a friend who sticks closer than a brother.
PROVERBS 18:24 ESV

Growing Hope

He has made everything beautiful in its time.

ECCLESIASTES 3:11 NKJV

Sometimes, life just falls apart. It's not that you haven't done a good job or haven't tried hard enough. It's not even that there is a remedy you have not yet discovered. It's just broken. You have nothing in your power to change this. You are stuck, and it's a mess.

How can trials like this possibly reconcile with God's message of hope and of His love for you?

Consider creation—plants in particular. Though a seed may lie dormant for years, there is still life inside. Even when it does spring forth, the seed itself dies. Yet slowly, new life sprouts from the source, undetected by the world above the soil. At just the right time, it becomes visible. And after a lot more time, it grows to produce fruit.

You and your life are in process. God has promised that He is at work in you to will and to do for His good pleasure

(Philippians 2:13). He has also promised that He is working everything for good because you love Him (Romans 8:28). God's track record on telling the truth is 100 percent. Like the seed beneath the soil, your circumstances may have you feeling trapped, lifeless, and without hope. Take heart! God who causes all things to be beautiful in its time is working a miracle into your story, too. Wait on Him. Draw nourishment from His living water. Rooted in His truth, you will watch God grow beauty in a place you never thought possible.

A wise gardener plants her seeds, then has the good sense not to dig them up every few days to see if a crop is on the way. Likewise, we must be patient as God brings the answers…in His own good time.

QUIN SHERRER

If anyone is in Christ, the new creation has come: The old has gone, the new is here!

2 CORINTHIANS 5:17 NIV

Secret Service

At Joppa there was a certain disciple named Tabitha, which is translated Dorcas. This woman was full of good works and charitable deeds which she did...and many believed on the LORD.

ACTS 9:36, 42 NKJV

As a kid, you had a parent or guardian for feedback. In school, you got a report card. Later, work rewarded effort with promotions or raises...or conversely, the threat of being fired if you didn't perform. No matter what the outcome, at least you knew where you stood, because you had a concrete measure of your effort's value.

But life everywhere else? How can you know if the day-in, day-out service you provide to your kids, spouse, church, friends, and community are worthwhile? Does changing a diaper, making a meal, or writing a letter actually matter in the big scheme of things?

Tabitha's story says yes. She served the Lord with all her heart by sewing garments for others. Making tunics might not sound very glamorous or even noteworthy. But God found her so impressive that after a sickness took her life and left her friends bereaved, he raised her from the dead! Her friends still needed her, and God showed in a most miraculous way that He valued her too. In the end, many believed in the Lord because of this humble seamstress.

Who knows if Tabitha ever got a "thank you" before the big event. Most people only miss kindness when it's no longer there. But God doesn't miss a thing. Every single smile you give, each hug wrapped to comfort, every piece of laundry folded is a fragrant offering of worship to Jesus, the greatest Servant of all. Your reward? An encounter with Jesus that changes you and the world.

Charity is never lost: it may meet with ingratitude, or be of no service to those on whom it was bestowed, yet it ever does a work of beauty and grace upon the heart of the giver.

CONYERS MIDDLETON

Your Father, who sees what is done in secret, will reward you.

MATTHEW 6:4 NIV

Chosen

*You didn't choose me. I chose you. I appointed you to
go and produce lasting fruit, so that the Father will
give you whatever you ask for, using my name.*

JOHN 15:16 NLT

Why do you think the Miss America pageant winner always
cries when they place the crown on her head? It seems like an
unusual response for such a grand and spectacular moment.

But that's exactly the point. That young lady knows full well
that there are many other worthy contestants who have beauty
and poise to rival her own. Yet she was chosen! The relief,
gratitude, and absolute thrill must be outstanding.

Now think about Jesus. Who chose Him to be crowned
King of the world? God, His Father. Who did He choose to
be His disciples? The famous twelve, with Matthias filling in
later. And who did the great King of kings choose to be in His
family? You! You, who have placed your trust in Jesus, have
been chosen to receive eternal love and divine inheritance,
crowned as a child of God and bride of Christ.

Was it something you said or did that drew His attention? Ephesians 1 says you were chosen in Christ before the foundation of the world. God simply knew and loved you before you ever said or did a thing. The day you received His Son, God opened the floodgates of blessing He had reserved just for you. Suddenly, crying for joy over such a spectacular moment makes perfect sense! Celebrate, because you are God's choice for His family.

God has a wonderful plan for each person He has chosen. He knew even before He created this world what beauty He would bring forth from our lives.

LOUISE B. WLY

He chose us in Him before the foundation of the world, that we should be holy and without blame before Him in love.

EPHESIANS 1:4–5 NKJV

At Home

God decided in advance to adopt us into his own
family by bringing us to himself through Jesus Christ.

EPHESIANS 1:5 NLT

What's the difference between the refrigerator at your
house and the one at your friend's? You feel more comfortable
opening your own.

It's not that your friend wouldn't gladly share his or her
food with you. But there are social norms to consider. Polite
constraints to uphold. It's always best to ask first—unless you're
at home. Then you can freely peruse the contents and eat to
your heart's delight without even a thought. It's one of the
perks of having your own place.

When you come before God, do you hesitate to take what
you need? Are you shy or reserved, either afraid to ask or
hoping your manners will win you what you want?

You are not a visitor. Because of Jesus, you are family, a
child of the King. With God, you are always home. As the best

Daddy and King ever, He has made His storehouse of richest treasure available to you whenever you want or need it. The Bible actually says He has given you every spiritual blessing in Christ. *It's all yours!* So forget the formalities and insecurities reserved for outsiders. In God's presence, you are free to talk and act and walk like one who is a dearly loved child—because that is who you are.

This is and has been the Father's work from the beginning— to bring us into the home of His heart.

GEORGE MACDONALD

See what great love the Father has lavished on us, that we should be called children of God! And that is what we are!

1 JOHN 3:1 NIV

Apple Delight

Show me the wonders of your great love...
Keep me as the apple of your eye;
hide me in the shadow of your wings.

PSALM 17:7–8 NKJV

What do you love more than anything in the world? God? Your family? Friends? Maybe a cool bowl of ice cream on a hot summer's day?

It's a hard question to answer sometimes because we use the word "love" so loosely. In the English language, the same word can be used to describe a million variations of desire for someone or something.

You might have heard the good news that God loves you. And it's true—the Bible says it over and over. But sometimes you can miss the true meaning. Looking at your track record, or maybe even deeper into your heart, you might conclude that while God may love you (because He doesn't lie), He couldn't possibly like you very much. So you resign yourself to, "At least I get to go to heaven, right?"

Friend, God doesn't just love you. He likes you. He delights in you. And He wants deep intimacy with you right now where you are, not just in heaven! So you don't miss the message, He repeats the theme again and again with all kinds of phrases. In Psalm 17 and again in Zechariah 2:8, you are the *apple of God's eye!* The one who brings the biggest smile to His face when He looks at you.

The next time you feel unnoticed, unloved, or unimportant, remember the truth. Your very life brightens the eyes of God who watches over you always, hiding you safely in the shadow of His wings.

As the beloved of God, under the shadow of His wings — and as the apple of God's eye — the seeds of great faith live within us.

GARY SMALLEY AND JOHN TRENT

He encircled him, he cared for him, he kept him as the apple of his eye.

DEUTERONOMY 32:10 ESV

Keep Connected

I am the vine, you are the branches. He who abides in Me, and
I in him, bears much fruit; for without Me you can do nothing.
JOHN 15:5 NKJV

Would you ever get mad at your three-year-old because he wouldn't help you fill out your tax forms? How absurd! No one would have such impossible expectations. They would go to someone who was trained and qualified for such work.

But do you ever get mad at yourself because you failed in an area you thought you should be able to handle by now, like that temper? That fly-off-the-handle mouth? That persistent worry? You confess and try harder. Then harder. Harder still, until you conclude it's no use. That sin is just going to stay.

Like trees in the wind, Jesus' words in John 15 remind you of a strength far greater than your own. He asks you to consider branches, and their ability to produce fruit. Dry and lifeless on the ground, they are powerless to produce anything. Connected to the vine, growth is inevitable. Just like you wouldn't expect a child to conjure wisdom outside his capacity, so you should rest from your frustration with sin, realizing you are powerless on your own to defeat it. Plug into Christ. Draw nourishment from His presence. Let His Word and Spirit renew your mind as you praise Him for His faithfulness. In time, you will see fruit. Not the contrived kind that doesn't last, but the genuine, life-giving sweetness that comes and stays through Christ.

Should we feel discouraged, a simple movement of heart toward God will renew our powers. Whatever He may demand of us, He will give us the strength and courage that we need.

FRANÇOIS FÉNELON

They are like trees planted
along the riverbank,
bearing fruit each season.
Their leaves never wither,
and they prosper in all they do.
PSALM 1:3 NLT

Christ's Fragrance

There is a sweet, wholesome fragrance in our lives. It is the fragrance of Christ within us, an aroma to both the saved and the unsaved all around us.

2 CORINTHIANS 2:15–16 TLB

Though new scents come out on the market all the time, perfume is as old as the hills. Literally, for thousands of years, people have produced fragrances because of the demand. Humans like to smell nice things! For whatever reason, God wired our brains to remember and respond to smells in a way unlike any of the other senses.

Since we are made in God's image, it isn't that surprising to discover that God likes to smell good things, too. Only, He isn't interested in what we can buy in the stores. God is sniffing out the Spirit of Christ in His children!

When you pray, God breathes it in. When you rejoice in His goodness, it deepens the aroma. When you love God and others, you have become a dispenser of Christ's exclusive fragrance. God detects His Son in you, and it pleases Him to no end.

Your divine fragrance floats beyond heaven. Its familiar scent strengthens the believers around you. And its lure draws the lost to its source.

Thank you for loving Jesus like you do. Everywhere you go, you fill the world with the beautiful aroma of Christ and His love.

The colored sunsets
and starry heavens, the
beautiful mountains
and the shining seas,
the fragrant woods and
painted flowers, are not
half so beautiful as a
soul that is serving Jesus
out of love.

FREDERICK W. FABER

Your name is like perfume poured out.

SONG OF SONGS 1:3 NIV

Out of Your Mind

Let everything that has breath praise the LORD! Praise the LORD!

PSALM 150:6 NIV

No one may be able to detect it by looking at you. All appearances say you're focused. Attentive. Productive. But inside your head, you have a secret operation happening. You're singing.

Maybe it's the last tune you heard before you turned off your car to head into work. The chorus you heard at church. Or some ditty from long ago that's been stuck in your head for a week. Occasionally, when your defenses are down in the shower or in your car and you think you're alone, the song breaks out of your mind, through your mouth, and into the open, giving the mental cage you've kept it in a little breathing space.

Whether or not you can carry a tune, God made you to sing. Not just in your head, but out loud for all of the world to hear. No need to worry about landing a record deal with anyone. He's not interested in pitch or musical perfection. God wants to hear your heart expressed in audible praise for Him.

Is the song of your soul one of thankfulness for who God is? Are you relieved your salvation is secure? That your sins are forgiven? That you have a future and a hope? If not, then confess it. If your mind is singing the wrong kind of lyrics, ask God to give you a new song. Then join the rest of creation as you belt out the joy of all who God is.

It is right and good that we, for all things, at all times, and in all places, give thanks and praise to You, O God. We worship You, we sing to You, and we give thanks to You: Maker, Nourisher, Guardian, Healer, Lord, and Father of all.

LANCELOT ANDREWES

O God, my heart is ready to praise you! I will sing and rejoice before you.

PSALM 108:1 TLB

Be still, and
listen to the
voice of your
heavenly Father.
His words can
renew your spirit.

Janet L. Smith

create

quiet moments

to exhale

with grace & gratitude

In the Gap

Therefore confess your sins to each other and pray for each other so that you may be healed. The prayer of a righteous person is powerful and effective.

JAMES 5:16 NIV

Peter's prospects were pretty grim. Authorities had already murdered James, John's brother, for following Jesus. Now Peter was imprisoned by the same hateful people, awaiting a similar fate. All the believers in the city were more than concerned. They wanted to help, but what could they do?

They could pray. They could gather together and ask God to help. And that's exactly what they did. While they huddled together in a house on the other side of town, standing in the gap for Peter, God sent an angel to set Peter free. When Peter arrived at the house where they were praying, they could hardly believe their eyes! Something amazing had just happened, and it had everything to do with God and their prayers.

What is burdening your heart today? What friend or coworker, family member or politician, pastor or missionary could use some help? Don't let prayer be your last recourse or the action for which you apologize, wishing you could help in some better way. Believer, prayer packs more power than any other effort you can give. God has blessed you with this privilege to change the course of history! He has called you to stand in the gap for those who are hurting and in need of Him. No authority or child or problem is beyond His reach. Like Peter's friends did, get together with other believers who look to the Lord for strength. Lift up your concerns before God's throne. Intercede for others, just as Jesus does for you. Then watch with amazement what God, your Father, will do through the power of your prayers!

Praying unlocks the doors of heaven and releases the power of God... Whether prayer changes our situation or not, one thing is certain: Prayer will change us!

BILLY GRAHAM

They all met together and were constantly united in prayer.

ACTS 1:14 NLT

Genuine Connection

Wake up, O LORD! Why do you sleep?
Get up! Do not reject us forever.

Wake up, O LORD! Why do you sleep?
Get up! Do not reject us forever.

PSALM 44:23 NLT

You and a family member have been going at it. Voices raised, tempers flared, and then the phone rings. Magically, your tone shifts as you answer, "Hello?" in a calm and kind voice. After all, why should you subject an innocent bystander to the darker side of your soul?

It's an unwritten social rule you learned when you were young. You have to be nice and keep up appearances no matter what's going on inside your heart and home. And so you think the same rule applies with God. Despite the turmoil in your soul, when you pray you automatically turn on the "nice voice." Make it pleasant, full of proper praise and petitions, because you don't want God to walk off.

The problem is, God doesn't want a fake you. He wants the real deal, sins and all. He wants you to come before Him in authentic dialogue, just like the psalmists always did. They voiced their deepest hurts and questions without pretense because they knew God already saw their souls. Laid out before Him, they trusted God to bear their pain and stand up under it. He promised to always hear and answer—and He did, time and time again.

What has been eating at you lately? What nagging question begs an answer? Ask your heavenly Father. Pour out your soul without fear of rejection, and expect an honest answer back from Him. Genuine relationship with God leads you out of theory into the reality of God's love and faithfulness toward you.

God desires authentic dialogue. As we speak what is on our hearts, we are sharing real information that God is deeply interested in.

RICHARD J. FOSTER

You do not take pleasure in burnt offerings.
My sacrifice, O God, is a broken spirit;
a broken and contrite heart you, God,
will not despise.

PSALM 51: 16–17 NIV

Safe and Secure

Then Peter came to himself and said, "Now I know without a doubt that the Lord has sent his angel and rescued me from Herod's clutches."
ACTS 12:11 NIV

Peter saw him with his own eyes, and still didn't understand what was happening. It wasn't until the angel left that he realized his chains were gone. Peter was free, and all of his friends' prayers had been answered.

You have to admit, you don't see angels anywhere either. Okay, maybe on greeting cards or lining a shelf in a home decor store. But real, bonafide angels? The kind that destroyed entire armies in the Old Testament, and almost always invoked fear whenever they appeared? Do they *really* exist?

In Ephesians 6, God tells us that every believer is a soldier in the middle of a cosmic spiritual war. You have an enemy whose sworn purpose is to destroy you—to rob you in any way he can from the joy, purpose, and hope that is yours in Jesus. But they're also the good guys. Angels whom Jesus, your

Commanding Officer, has ordered to your side for protection, to guard you in all your ways. And He has given you special, spiritual armor uniquely designed to protect your heart, mind, and body. The ground on which you fight is belief.

Do you believe that you are not alone? That not only Jesus stands with you, but the myriad of angels at His disposal do, too? You have more reasons than you can see to be strong and courageous. You have an unseen world of warriors waiting to help you at your side.

God is constantly taking knowledge of me in love and watching over me for my good.

J. I. PACKER

Angels are God's representatives...They protect us time after time in ways we are not even aware of.

HOPE MACDONALD

For he will command his angels concerning you to guard you in all your ways.

PSALM 91:11 NRSV

Think Again

How precious to me are your thoughts, God!
How vast is the sum of them!
Were I to count them,
they would outnumber the grains of sand.

PSALM 139:17–18 NIV

You see it in the movies all the time. A couple falls in love. He is absolutely infatuated with her. She can't stop thinking about him. They are obsessed and delighted by even the thought of each other. It's just the way love goes.

Believe it or not, romance didn't start in Hollywood. The idea began with God, the author of love. Your view of that love, though, gets distorted in a myriad of ways, broken by a sinful world. But every now and then, in the purity of unadulterated affection, you see a glimpse of what real love looks like...a taste of just how passionate God feels—about you.

Psalm 139 lets you know that the God who made you loves you more than you could ever imagine. He knows when you sit down and get up, where you go to sleep and when you rise.

He even knows what you're going to think before you think it! He protects you, plans for you, and cares for you.

More than that, God thinks about you all of the time. Before the world was made, you were on His mind. While you were being knitted together inside your mom, He was thinking about you. In fact, the psalmist says that if you tried to count how many thoughts God has about you, you could never do it. You wouldn't have enough time!

Now that's the heart of romance. Even Hollywood can't hold a candle to it.

The God who created, names, and numbers the stars in the heavens also numbers the hairs of my head...He pays attention to very big things and to very small ones. What matters to me matters to Him, and that changes my life.

ELISABETH ELLIOT

He pays... attention to you, down to the last detail even numbering the hairs on your head!

MATTHEW 10:30 MSG

In Hot Pursuit

Draw me after you and let us run together!
The king has brought me into his chambers.

SONG OF SOLOMON 1:4 NASB

It's that feeling you get when the phone rings and you know it's him, the one you've been waiting for. Answering, you're delighted to discover he wants a date. *He wants to be with you.* It doesn't matter if you have been married to him for fifty years or still in the dating stage. Nothing compares to the joy of being pursued by the one you love.

There's no getting around it. You are wired for connection. While social media in the modern age handles the looser communal needs you feel, each person longs for a deeper, richer, truer place of intimacy. You want to know and be known. To receive and give real love.

God knows exactly how you feel. Not only did He create you that way, He feels that way Himself. That's why He made you with those desires. And that's why, since the beginning of time, He has pursued a relationship with you, to give you what you desire most in Himself.

The Song of Solomon captures God's epic love story with you in a poetic allegory. A king and a Shulamite girl fall in love. Despite their status inequality, he pursues her with fixed determination, and she responds with echoed longing. In the end, they are united in marriage—desire consummated by intimate connection and life-long commitment.

Whether or not someone's texting, messaging, or calling on you, you are being pursued by the greatest love of your life. Let the loneliness that this world often brings drive you into the arms of your loving Lord who waits to receive you. More than that, who pursues you until you feel the full impact of His unending love.

What extraordinary delight we find in the presence of God. He draws us in, His welcome so fresh and inviting.

I am my beloved's,
And my beloved
is mine.

SONG OF SOLOMON 6:3 NKJV

Future Promise

"For I know the plans I have for you," declares the LORD, "plans to prosper you and not to harm you, plans to give you a hope and a future."
JEREMIAH 29:11 NIV

Think back to a time when you felt totally safe and secure. What is the difference between that memory and your current reality? Chances are, the discrepancy between the two lay in whom you were with and how much you knew about the world. As a child, you trusted that someone was going to take care of everything. As an adult, you're not so sure.

Truth is, the more you experience life, the more you see. Wonderful, joyful blessings spring up in the most unlikely places—but so dopain and suffering. It's the not knowing what's going to come next that ushers out our childlike faith and escorts us into fear and worry.

Even though God never promises His children a trial-free life (in fact, Scripture says to expect suffering), you can face the future with hope and joy. Why? Because God *has* promised to use every moment of your life for your good. Nothing is wasted, even the darkest days that seem to have no purpose or good in them at all. Remember your childlike trust, and place it in the One who is worthy to receive it. He is planning so much good for you, your mind cannot even conceive it. Seek Him with all your heart, and He will give you what you'll desire most: Him.

God has not promised skies always blue,
flower-strewn pathways all our lives through;
God has not promised sun without rain,
joy without sorrow, peace without pain.
But God has promised strength for the day,
rest for the labor, light for the way,
grace for the trials,
help from above,
unfailing sympathy, undying love.

ANNIE JOHNSON FLINT

"No eye has seen, nor ear heard, nor the heart of man imagined, what God has prepared for those who love him."

1 CORINTHIANS 2:9 ESV

God Advice

Simon Peter answered him, "Lord, to whom
shall we go? You have the words of eternal life."

JOHN 6:68 NIV

You can find it on TV, if you're looking for it. The radio boasts its own spectrum of opinions, too, allowing you to tune in to whatever political, philosophical, or team affiliation you have. Throw in the millions of books written on every topic imaginable and you'd have to conclude: the culture is saturated with advice.

The problem is, who is right?

Post-modern theorists try to simplify the answer. "Everybody is. You just create your own reality and live the best you can in it," they assert. Jesus, however, says otherwise. Offensive as He may sound in an everything-is-included culture, Jesus' position on truth is quite exclusive. He says, "I am the way and the truth and the life. No one comes to the Father except through Me" (John 14:6).

In fact, Jesus spoke many difficult words that troubled even His followers. Some of them left as a result. When Jesus asked Peter if he'd like to leave, too, Peter's answer was classic, "Lord, to whom shall we go? You have the words of eternal life."

As the people around you clamor for direction and wise counsel, don't cower under political correctness, or shy away from what Scripture clearly says. Because of Jesus, you have the power to bring life to others by speaking God's truth and showing them the way to God's heart. It is the gospel of Christ that is the power of God for salvation to those who believe.

When the world around us staggers from lack of direction, God offers purpose, hope, and certainty.

GLORIA GAITHER

Recognizing who we are in Christ and aligning our life with God's purpose for us gives a sense of destiny... It gives form and direction to our life.

JEAN FLEMING

Knowing God results in every other kind of understanding.

PROVERBS 9:10 TLB

Wrapped Up

I am overwhelmed with joy in the LORD my God!
For he has dressed me with the clothing of salvation
and draped me in a robe of righteousness.
I am like a bridegroom in his wedding suit
or a bride with her jewels.

ISAIAH 61:10 NLT

First come the flower girls, and you know it's about to happen. One by one, bridesmaids and groomsmen slowly walk down the aisle, setting the perfect stage. Suddenly, the music shifts. Everyone stands. The bride has entered the room...and she's headed for her groom.

The flowers, the purity, the promise of love and future—it's hard for anyone to keep from crying. Few things in life are as beautiful as two people committing their lives to live as one.

You, dear friend, have a wedding day in store for you unlike any you have seen or experienced on this earth. God the Father has chosen a bride. As a believer, you are betrothed to His Son.

Where can you possibly find clothes appropriate for such an occasion? Don't worry. Jesus will wrap you in His own spotless robe, perfectly fit for the occasion of being wed to Christ. Every test and trial of your faith now is adding to your beauty to be revealed on that incredible day. When it finally arrives, all the planning and preparing, even the pain and the waiting, will quickly be forgotten as you stare into the eyes of the One who has loved you from before time began.

God is seeking you...
He is the Lover, and
you are His beloved.
He has promised
Himself to you.

JOHN OF THE CROSS

Clothe yourself
with the presence
of the Lord
Jesus Christ.

ROMANS 13:14 NLT

One Love

For God so loved the world that he gave his one and only Son,
that whoever believes in him shall not perish but have eternal life.

JOHN 3:16 NIV

It's easy to picture the face of love when you think of Jesus and all that He did. The humility of God being born in a stable, cradled in a manger. The unassuming childhood, growing up learning His father's trade, as any teen boy would. Then His years of ministry, a life poured out for other people. Constantly serving, loving, meeting needs at their deepest place. Then sacrificing His life to satisfy the wrath of God.

The wrath of God. Anger. Death. Suddenly, part of the gospel story doesn't compute. You take a look at the Old Testament and God, at first glance, seems so different from His Son. Harsh. Strict. Severe. These words come to mind instead. It becomes easy to believe Jesus loves us, but hard to believe the Father ever would.

But when you miss the Father's love, you miss the point of

Jesus. Jesus and the Father are one. To know one is to know the other. Everything Jesus ever did was an expression of obedience to what His Father asked—especially death on the cross. Then the Father showed His ultimate approval of Christ's sacrifice by raising Him from the dead and seating Jesus on His throne in heaven forever.

The famous John 3:16 verse captures God the Father's heart for you, as evidenced through Jesus. Sin is a separator and must be remedied because of God's righteousness. But God, at tremendous personal cost, willingly gave what was most precious to Him in order to win you back.

The Breadth: God so loved the world
The Length: that He gave His
only begotten Son
The Depth: that whosoever believeth
on Him shall not perish
The Height: but shall have
everlasting life.

I and the Father are one.
JOHN 10:30 NIV

plant

seeds

kindnes

watc

Goodnes

grow & gr

Friendship
is the fruit
gathered from
the trees
planted in
the rich soil
of love, and
nurtured with
tender care and
understanding.

Alma L. Weixelbaum

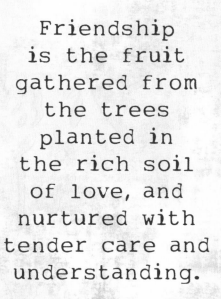

The Anchor

*Ruth replied, "Don't urge me to leave you or to turn back
from you. Where you go I will go, and where you stay I will
stay. Your people will be my people and your God my God."*

RUTH 1:16 NIV

It looked like they had lost everything. Naomi's husband
had already died. Now her two sons were dead, too, leaving
Ruth and Orpah, their widows, wondering what to do next.
Naomi tried to convince them to leave. "Go back home where
you have a chance at finding a husband," she urged. Orpah
agreed. But clinging to her mother-in-law, Ruth left her home
in Moab to build a new one with Naomi among God's people.

Why? Through her relationship with these Israelites, Ruth
encountered truth. With Naomi, she learned about the God of
Israel. She realized that no matter what trials life would bring,
if she had God and His people, she had everything she needed.

The same holds true for you. Experience tells you that hard
times come for all people. Sometimes it feels like you've lost

everything. But Ruth's determination to stay with Naomi tells you there is one truth left to grasp. God alone is your anchor, your home. Like Ruth, you have to hold onto God and His people, even if it means letting go of the life you once knew. It can be scary to trust a God you can't see, not knowing what will come next. But God, who knows the future, has wonderful plans for you. Staying in fellowship with Him and His people through life's storms is the surest path to future peace.

God is always present in the temple of your heart...His home. And when you come in to meet Him there, you find that it is the one place of deep satisfaction where every longing is met.

My grace is sufficient for you, for my power is made perfect in weakness.

2 CORINTHIANS 12:9 NIV

Again

The steadfast love of the LORD never ceases,
his mercies never come to an end;
they are new every morning;
great is your faithfulness.
"The LORD is my portion," says my soul,
"therefore I will hope in him."

LAMENTATIONS 3:22–24 NRSV

Ugh. You just did it again for what seems like the millionth time. *How many times am I going to keep making that same mistake?* you agonize in your head. Sheepishly, you try to duck the knowing gaze of your heavenly Father, keeping yourself busy, trying to put more good works into the equation before you look His direction. *What if this was the last straw, and His patience with me runs out?* you fear.

Dear friend, God's ways simply don't equal ours. Though your parents, friends, spouse, kids, or boss may run out of mercy, your heavenly Father does not. He promises you that

74

His mercies are new every morning because of His great faithfulness, not your stellar performance. You can never mess up more than His love can cover. Simply come to Him and receive the forgiveness you desperately need and His loving Spirit to strengthen your love for Him. In time, you will see the kindness of God work wonders in your soul, freeing you from the habits of sin you once knew. Forgiven and freed, you can offer the same patience and hope to others around you who need God's love, too.

Have confidence in God's mercy, for when you think He is a long way from you, He is often quite near.

THOMAS À KEMPIS

"Lord, how many times shall I forgive...? Up to seven times?" Jesus answered, "I tell you, not seven times, but seventy-seven times."

MATTHEW 18:22 NIV

A Reasonable Offer

"Come now, and let us reason together," says the LORD, "Though your sins are as scarlet, they will be as white as snow."

ISAIAH 1:18 NASB

Your child is sitting on the park bench, arms crossed. The girl she was playing with is sulking on the swings. "What happened?" you ask, surmising the problem. "Why don't you want to play?" After your daughter pours out her heart, you gently walk her over to the other child. Then you start to reason with them both. "Don't you girls want to play together? Can you say you're sorry so that you can start having fun again?" you counsel.

It's amazing how much the playground mirrors adult life. Though grown and supposedly mature, we adults still manage to get frustrated with others, threatening to shut down until further notice. You don't like the way life is playing out, and you just want to get mad and sit down.

Then God, the ultimate parent, approaches the scene.

Unlike other people, God invites reason—together. There is no need for hiding, sulking, or staying away. No use for martyrdom, complaining, or whining. God your Father has demonstrated His solution: true forgiveness. Now all things work together for your good. Life has meaning and purpose, and promises to be the grandest adventure if you will just stand back up and get in the game.

Do you know of someone else who is giving up on life? As your Father does with you, reason with them. Remind them of the hope that comes through a real relationship with Him. Invite them to join you as you enjoy life lived in God's goodness.

Forgiveness is not acting as if things are just the same as before the offense. We must face the fact that things will never be the same. By the grace of God they can be a thousand times better, but they will never again be the same.

RICHARD J. FOSTER

May the God of hope fill you with all joy and peace as you trust in him.

ROMANS 15:13

Bolder Service

Be strong and courageous! Do not tremble or be dismayed,
for the LORD your God is with you wherever you go.

JOSHUA 1:9 NASB

Some people just seem to have it. Whether it's the pastor at
church, the politician on the news, or the movie stars on the big
screen, it seems that God has just gifted some people with the
ability to lead, speak, and get things done. They are the movers
and shakers.

You, however, are the servant-heart—the person who
quietly works behind the scenes making life better for others,
content to only read about the exploits of the adventurous.

Certainly, God loves to see His people humbly serving
others. The problem comes when we need to speak but cower
in quietness instead. In an effort to keep the boat from rocking,
we may miss the ship God is sailing altogether. God didn't put
His Spirit inside you so that you could hide His light behind
your shyness. He wants you, like His servant Joshua, to be bold

and brave! Strong and courageous! The mover and shaker in the lives of the people He has placed around you.

It doesn't mean you have to lead the masses like God calls some to do. But it does mean listening to His Spirit and being obedient to whatever He asks you to do. Are you to pray out loud with that person next to you? Should you finally share your testimony with your coworker? It may seem scary at first, like the first drop of a roller coaster. But before you know it, you'll be amazed at the incredible ride God's planned for you. Just like Joshua who led God's people to spectacular victory, you will be used of God in amazing ways when you step out of your comfort zone into faith.

Faith in God gives your life a center from which you can reach out and dare to love the world.

BARBARA FARMER

God doesn't want us to be shy with his gifts, but bold and loving and sensible.

2 TIMOTHY 1:7 MSG

On Your Side

If God is for us, who can be against us?

ROMANS 8:31 NIV

You've seen it played out on the football field. Players who are supposed to be gearing up for the next play suddenly turn to face the crowd. Throwing their hands up and up, you realize they're sending a signal to you, the fans. *Get louder! Cheer us on! Distract our opposition!* they're telling you. And somehow, simply by hearing and knowing that people are for them, momentum changes. They get the ball back, drive it down the field, and score.

It just helps to know that you're not alone in your efforts. That someone believes in you, is for you, and is cheering you on.

God wants you to know He is your greatest fan. He has studied your plays and knows your routine. He knows what energizes you, and what gets you down. He reads you better than any playbook. You are a star on His team, and He wants you to win every time.

So ignore the jeers from the opposing side. Listen for the voice of God who has equipped you to walk in victory, who cheers you on, no matter how many times you may fumble the ball. If God is for you, who can be against you? God doesn't have any losers on His team. He has made you the victor through the Lord Jesus Christ.

Grasp the fact that God is for you—let this certainty make its impact on you in relation to what you are up against at this very moment; and you will find in thus knowing God as your sovereign protector...both freedom from fear and new strength for the fight.

J. I. PACKER

My help comes from the LORD, the Maker of heaven and earth.
PSALM 121:2 NIV

Pointed Pruning

Consider it pure joy...whenever you face trials of many kinds, because you know that the testing of your faith produces perseverance. Let perseverance finish its work so that you may be mature and complete, not lacking anything.
JAMES 1:2–4 NIV

You know that person...the one who can't seem to keep from irritating you down to the core. Under normal circumstances, you can keep a cool demeanor. But this person is just different, like they were born to bother you. *I'd be a much better Christian if this character weren't in my life*, you think to yourself.

But have you ever stopped to consider that God put *that character* into your life on purpose? That maybe you have some core issues that can't be addressed without someone just like him or her bringing it up to the surface?

Friend, there is more than one reason why Paul says to consider trials a joy. God uses the painful circumstances in your life to prune the branches that are blocking your growth.

Without that necessary work in your life, you'd fail to grow into all God intends for you to be.

The next time your nemesis comes near and your nerves start to prickle, stop whatever you're doing and thank God for the work He is doing in you. Ask Him for a heart like His, one that loves others even at its own expense. Surrender to the pruning and watch with expectation at the abundant fruit that will soon bloom right at the stripping point.

Be open to the pruning in you life. All growing things bloom more beautifully after they're pruned.

JOY WISEHART

Every branch that does bear fruit
he prunes so that it will be even
more fruitful.

JOHN 15:2 NIV

Together Forever

I am convinced that nothing can ever separate us from God's love. Neither death nor life, neither angels nor demons, neither our fears for today nor our worries about tomorrow—not even the powers of hell can separate us from God's love.

ROMANS 8:38 NLT

It's why parents panic when they can't find their kids. Why lovers give each other rings and make lasting promises. Why people get so sad when someone dies.

People were created to stay together. We never want to lose the ones who are closest to us. But in a world riddled with the effects of sin, separation happens in a myriad of ways. Heartbreaking loss, time and again, hurts enough to make you pull back. To convince you not to put yourself out there any more. To choose no love at all instead of love at risk of loss.

Dear friend, bring your wounds to Jesus. Even He wept at the loss of his close friend, Lazarus. He knows separation hurts. Let him wipe the tears from your eyes and comfort you with His own faithful presence. Then reflect on His outstanding promise to you: nothing can separate you from the love of God in Christ Jesus! Just to drive the point home in Romans 8, Paul lists out a host of dramatic events that under normal circumstances would certainly tear people apart. But God's love is greater than anything else in creation. And by His power, He will always keep you close to Him, *no matter what!* Let God's promise of unfailing love strengthen your weary soul so you can keep living full and large, risking your all for the sake of His love.

Dare to love and to be a real friend. The love you give and receive is a reality that will lead you closer and closer to God as well as to those whom God has given you to love.

HENRI J. M. NOUWEN

I give them eternal life, and they shall never perish; no one will snatch them out of my hand.

JOHN 10:28 NIV

Body Language

For even as the body is one and yet has many members, and all the members of the body, though they are many, are one body, so also is Christ.

1 Corinthians 12:12 NASB

Have you ever seen an eyeball working on its own?

Gross.

No, eyes look much better when situated on a face. And hands work so much better when attached to arms, and arms to bodies. Though you may not like all the ways your body parts fit together, you have to agree that its much better when they are connected.

Have you ever heard that you are a body part? That's what God says. At least, that's one of the ways He describes His people. He has made each of His children in a unique way that is designed to connect with the others so that together—and only together—they can function as the body of Jesus Christ, whose Spirit gives life to the members. Even though other believers can be flat out irritating at times, as part of the same body, we have to have each other.

So how is your body language? Are you connected, pulsing with the flow of the Spirit, moving in the way you were designed? Or have you separated yourself, convinced of your inadequacy or filled with frustration at others? The best connection happens first with the head—Jesus. As you get His bearings, bring yourself into full body connection. Watch how your unique contribution will bless those around you and bring new life to the body!

Yours are the eyes through which Christ's compassion for the world is to look out; yours are the feet with which He is to go about doing good; and yours are the hands with which He is to bless us now.

TERESA OF ÁVILA

Out of the generosity of Christ, each of us is given his own gift.

EPHESIANS 4:7 MSG

Pit Stop

We know how dearly God loves us, because he has given us the Holy Spirit to fill our hearts with his love.

ROMANS 5:5 NLT

Have you ever run out of gas on the interstate? Cruising along, headed for your next destination when your car starts lurching. You check and notice the little red needle way below the E. *Now why didn't I see that coming?* you wonder as your car slows to a stop.

In many ways, your spiritual life is a lot like your car. It is designed to run on the fuel of God's Holy Spirit who empowers you to say and do all that God has planned for you that day. So why is it, then, that your energy feels so drained these days? The activities that once brought you joy now bog you down. Like your car, your life has come to a dead stop.

It's time to check your gauges. Have you been filling your days with to-do lists that start at your clock's alarm and continue until your head hits the pillow again? If so, you are running on empty because you haven't stopped long enough to fill up with God's presence. Jesus said that as a branch can produce no fruit if it is detached from the vine, so you cannot hope to live life—a meaningful, joy-filled life—apart from His Spirit. The good news is that Jesus offers rest to the weary. All you need to do is make a daily pit stop. Start sitting at His feet, soaking in the truth of His Word, and let His Spirit wash away the muck of self-effort that clogs your soul. He will pour His love into your heart, refueling you to run with joy and His energy—the way you were designed.

Grace is an energy...as real an energy as the energy of electricity... rolling in plenteousness toward the shores of human need.

BENJAMIN JOWETT

Blessed are those who hunger
and thirst for righteousness,
for they will be filled.
MATTHEW 5:6 NIV

God created us
with an overwhelming
desire to soar...
realistically dreaming
of what He can do
with our potential.

Carol Kent

His love lifts us
to a higher beauty.

Battle Gear

We are not fighting against flesh-and-blood enemies, but against evil rulers and authorities of the unseen world....Therefore, put on every piece of God's armor so you will be able to resist the enemy.

EPHESIANS 6:12–13 NLT

Every morning you roll out of bed and head to the bathroom. Yes, there it is, the mirror with your disheveled reflection in it. Already you know the drill: Brush teeth, take a shower, find an outfit, fix your hair, and brace yourself for the day's tasks you can already hear calling your name.

One of those voices you hear, though—the still, small, quiet one—is God's Spirit vying for your attention. It seems that in the tyranny of the urgent or the monotony of the seemingly mundane, you've forgotten the true state of affairs. When you rise to face another day, you're stepping back into a spiritual battle raging around you. God warns you that the unseen forces of evil bent on your destruction stand ready to attack and drag you to the ground. Without proper protection, your mind and spirit won't stand a chance.

The commander of Heaven's armies, Jesus Himself, has given you the spiritual armor you need to win the day's battle. The belt of truth, breastplate of righteousness, shoes of peace, shield of faith, helmet of salvation, and the sword of the Spirit are each designed to not only protect you, but empower you to take down enemy strongholds by God's Spirit. Each piece is a part of your relationship with Jesus who is your defender and Savior. Take time today to strengthen yourself in Him. Clothe yourself with His presence, and take on the day with a new determination—victory and glory in Christ!

He is the Source. Of everything. Strength for your day. Wisdom for your task....Grace for your battle. Provision for each need... Assistance for every encounter.

JACK HAYFORD

I have fought the good fight,
I have finished the race,
I have kept the faith.

2 TIMOTHY 4:7 NIV

Heaven's Pedicure

How beautiful on the mountains are the feet of those who bring good news,
who proclaim peace, who bring good tidings, who proclaim salvation.

Isaiah 52:7 NIV

Have you ever had a pedicure, one of those lavish kind where they lather your feet and legs with wonderful lotions and salts, then rub the stress and callouses of the day away? It seems like so much fanfare for feet, the often-overlooked-but-so-necessary part of our bodies. You have to admit, even after a good buff and paint job, they still look rather odd.

But not to God! He says your feet are beautiful, pedicure or not. It's not the treatment you give them that makes it so. It's their function, and the places they take you.

Your heavenly Father has given you feet to walk you into other people's lives. They carry you into places where people are hungry for God, desperately needing His love and truth. You, as God's child, have everything that they need to hear about a relationship with Jesus. God says that when you walk out of your comfort zone to carry the good news of His Son to another person, you are beautiful, from your head to your toes. It's just what happens when God's love fills you and you are faithful to walk where He leads you.

In the morning let our hearts gaze upon God's love and the love He has allowed us to share, and in the beauty of that vision, let us go forth to meet the day.

ROY LESSIN

Jesus wants to live His life in you, to look through your eyes, walk with your feet, love with your heart.

MOTHER TERESA

Stand firm then...with your feet fitted with the readiness that comes from the gospel of peace.

EPHESIANS 6:14-15 NIV

Called to Action

He who calls you is faithful; he will surely do it.

1 THESSALONIANS 5:24 ESV

Moses knew the Israelites would ask. After all, he had been hiding out in Midian as a shepherd for forty years, avoiding all his responsibilities back in Egypt. What right did he have to march back in and act like a leader who could take those people out of slavery and into a new land altogether?

From Moses' perspective, God had picked the wrong person. "I'm not even a good speaker," he retorted back to the God who made his tongue.

Of course, as you read the story from the comfort of your chair, you're apt to chide Moses. *How can you argue with God like that? Don't you know if He tells you to do something, He'll make it work out?*

You sit astounded with Moses' stubbornness, until God's Spirit turns your gaze inward. What has God asked you to do today that makes you quake with fear? Forgive that person who has wronged you so many times? Give up that job promotion so you can spend more time with your family? What has kept you immobilized so far?

Don't second-guess yourself like Moses did. You always will if your perspective stops with you. You have been called to action by a God who stands right by your side. Better still, His Spirit fills you with the power to change lives—your own and the others around you. Like Moses, you must learn to trust—not in what you can do but in who God is. He is faithful to provide everything you need for all He has called you to do.

Each of us may be sure that if God sends us on stony paths He will provide us with strong shoes, and He will not send us out on any journey for which He does not equip us well.

ALEXANDER MACLAREN

Let us hold
unswervingly to
the hope we profess,
for he who promised
is faithful.
HEBREWS 10:23 NIV

The Salt Solution

You are the salt of the earth, but if salt has lost
its taste, how shall its saltiness be restored?

MATTHEW 5:13 ESV

The clouds break and a shaft of light beams down, lighting
the package on your table. McDonald's french fries—the
ultimate in fried potato excellence—beckons to your waiting
taste buds. You pop a few in your mouth, but your eyebrows
furrow. You are concerned. Taking a few more bites, you realize
no one salted your batch. What was supposed to be wonderful
are just greasy sticks of bland potato, lacking the pleasure they
had promised to bring.

Even if you don't really like salty things, God says His
people can learn a lot from the mineral. Salt has a unique
ability to bring out flavor wherever it is applied. It's also used to
preserve. And He wants you to be just like that salt.

Unlike people who don't know Jesus, you have been
seasoned with His precious Holy Spirit. The flavor of God
filters through all that you do, whether you're waiting in the

carpool line, working your job, or wandering through the grocery store. Wherever you go, God's goodness goes with you. So when you encounter other people, there's nothing bland about the exchange if you give others a taste of that goodness. Conversations carried through God's Spirit create a thirst for God and preserve what is true—the inevitable effect of a good salting.

So how salty are you? It depends on how well connected you are to the Source. Go to God today and let His Spirit refresh your soul. Reflect on His power to love and preserve you. Then sprinkle the love of God wherever you go.

Begin today! No matter how feeble the light, let it shine as best it may. The world may need just that quality of light which you have.

HENRY C. BLINN

Let your conversation be always full of grace, seasoned with salt, so that you may know how to answer everyone.

COLOSSIANS 4:6 NIV

Carried

He tends his flock like a shepherd:
He gathers the lambs in his arms
and carries them close to his heart;
he gently leads those that have young.

ISAIAH 40:11 NIV

You probably haven't watched any sheep lately. Truth is, shepherding isn't one of the top occupations most places. Even in Bible times, shepherds weren't often shown the most respect. But theirs is a needed service, and their work forms the greatest spiritual analogy for Jesus and His people.

You, God says, are His sheep. Jesus is your great Shepherd. What does a shepherd do? He cares for His sheep. Not like some hired hand whose heart isn't in it. The Good Shepherd devotes His entire life to His sheep because these are His. He knows them by name and they know His voice. He leads them, guides them—especially those that are with young. He takes them to where the water runs clean and the pastures burst with vibrant, nourishing greens. He doesn't just want His flock to live, He aims for them to thrive under His gentle, expert care.

Little lamb, do you ever feel lost or afraid? Do you feel like the demands of life are too great for you to handle? Are you confused about which way to turn? Listen for the sound of your Shepherd's voice calling out to you. He is with you, leading and protecting you. You cannot fall into harm's way when you are following after Him. And when your strength is gone, lie down and let Him carry you in His arms.

God never abandons anyone on whom He has set His love; nor does Christ, the good shepherd, ever lose track of His sheep.

J. I. PACKER

Then Jesus said, "Come to me, all of you who are weary and carry heavy burdens, and I will give you rest."

MATTHEW 11:28 NIV

Prayer Offering

Another angel...was given much incense to offer with the prayers of
all the saints on the golden altar before the throne, and the smoke of
the incense, with the prayers of the saints, rose before God.

REVELATION 8:3–4 ESV

Imagine the end of the world. Jesus, the triumphant Lamb of God, stands ready to claim the people who are rightfully His, and rid the world of sin and shame forever. As you behold this heavenly scene, your eyes take note of a curious bowl sitting before God's throne from which you smell the most fragrant aroma to ever grace your senses. *What is the source of this magnificent scent?* you wonder as you peer inside.

Prayers! Hundreds of thousands of saintly prayers pour forth their fragrance to God in unparalleled worship. It is a glimpse into God's heart, and what He truly holds dear.

You may have never thought of your prayers as incense, a sacrifice of worship to God, but the book of Revelation shows us they are. God cares so much about what you have to say that

He saves every word in His altar of incense where the cries of your heart rise before His presence continually.

Dear child of God, never believe the lie that prayer doesn't work or God isn't listening. The truth is, every word you whisper finds its place right before the Father. He will answer with His wisdom and in His time to every call you make. May John's vision of the purpose and power of prayer persuade you to bend your knees more often as you call out to the Lord.

A saint is never consciously a saint; a saint is consciously dependent on God.

OSWALD CHAMBERS

The world may doubt the power of prayer. But the saints know better.

GILBERT SHAW

May my prayer be set before you like incense; may the lifting up of my hands be like the evening sacrifice.

PSALM 141:2 NIV

Kingdom Keys

Do not be afraid, little flock, for your Father
has been pleased to give you the kingdom.

LUKE 12:32 NIV

The doorbell rings. You check to see who's standing at the door, and you notice a television crew standing behind a man with lots of balloons. Out of curiosity, you crack the door open. "Congratulations!" everyone outside cries. "You are our next million-dollar sweepstakes winner!"

How would you react? Would that news change your life?

When you chose to put your faith in Jesus Christ, something far better than winning a contest happened. You were handed a glorious kingdom filled with the richest treasures that will never go away. Jesus says every blessing you will ever need to live a joy-filled, satisfied life is yours for the taking now that you have been adopted into His royal family.

Are you afraid and need peace to calm your fears? He offers it freely. Are you concerned about finances and how you will provide for your family? The King has promised to provide. Have the pressures of life weighed you down? God's Spirit will lift you up. Even though sin and the effects of sin still wreak havoc in your world, you no longer have to be afraid. You are not an orphan anymore. God, your heavenly Daddy and King, has never failed to meet the needs of His kids. He is delighted to give you the whole kingdom in Christ.

God is waiting for us to come to Him with our needs...God's throne room is always open... Every single believer in the whole world could walk into the throne room all at one time, and it would not even be crowded.

CHARLES STANLEY

Seek the Kingdom of God above all else, and live righteously, and he will give you everything you need.

MATTHEW 6:33 NLT

The Secret Place

Many of the Samaritans from that town believed in him because of the woman's testimony, "He told me everything I ever did."

JOHN 4:39 NIV

How'd you like to meet a stranger who knew all your deepest secrets? Would it be a bit unnerving? The Samaritan woman who encountered Jesus at the well probably thought so. Without divulging any personal information, she listened to Jesus recount her life story—and she was amazed.

Amazed that a Jewish man would defy custom and rank to speak with a lowly Samaritan woman. Shocked that He knew so much detailed information about her. And delightfully surprised to discover He didn't hate her because of what He knew. In fact, He challenged her to live bigger and better. To stop drinking from the tainted wells of life that don't satisfy, and to quench her thirst for real abundant life in Him, the promised Savior!

She couldn't keep it in. She ran to tell the entire city what this incredible man had said and done. Without knowing it or even trying, this Samaritan woman became the first female missionary who won her town to Christ.

It's the kind of thing that happens whenever you truly encounter Jesus and allow Him access to the secret places of your soul. He isn't surprised or repulsed by what He finds. Instead, He has a way of knowing, forgiving, and healing unlike anything else in this world. Once you've tasted of His living water, you—like the Samaritan woman—will never thirst again, and the world will never be the same.

Drink deeply from the very Source the deep calm and peace of interior quietude and refreshment of God, allowing the pure water of divine grace to flow plentifully and unceasingly from the Source itself.

MOTHER TERESA

Whoever drinks the water I give them will never thirst. Indeed, the water I give them will become in them a spring of water welling up to eternal life.

JOHN 4:14 NIV

Different

Ye are a chosen generation, a royal priesthood, an holy nation,
a peculiar people; that ye should shew forth the praises of him
who hath called you out of darkness into his marvellous light.

1 Peter 2:9 KJV

You couldn't miss them. Led by pillars of cloud and fire,
fed by raining manna, and empowered by unseen angels, the
Israelites had developed quite a reputation for themselves
wherever they travelled. In a word, they were different. Set
apart from all the other nations. Holy, because God the Creator
lived among them.

In Christ, you are every bit as weird as those Israelites felt
back then. Okay, weird may sound extreme, but it's how you
may feel in the midst of a culture that criticizes Jesus Christ and
anyone who follows Him. Jesus says you are more than okay in
your weirdness. He has called you to be a "peculiar people."
You are to stand out from the non-believers in such a dramatic
way that they will beg to know what makes you tick. Then you

can tell them that God's Spirit within you sets you apart.

What does "different" look like? Is it what you eat or don't eat? Drink or don't drink? Say or don't say? All these areas may be affected, but the defining difference between God's people and others is His Spirit dwelling inside you. The more we obey His Spirit's lead, the more others will see God's unconditional love, joy, peace, patience, kindness, goodness, faithfulness, gentleness, and self-control. In other words, they will see the fruit of God's Spirit in you, and that difference in you will make all the difference in the world.

I am wholly His; I am peculiarly His; I am universally His; I am eternally His.

THOMAS BENTON BROOKS

Embracing what God does for you is the best thing you can do for him. Don't become so well-adjusted to your culture...Instead, fix your attention on God. You'll be changed from the inside out.

ROMANS 12:2 MSG

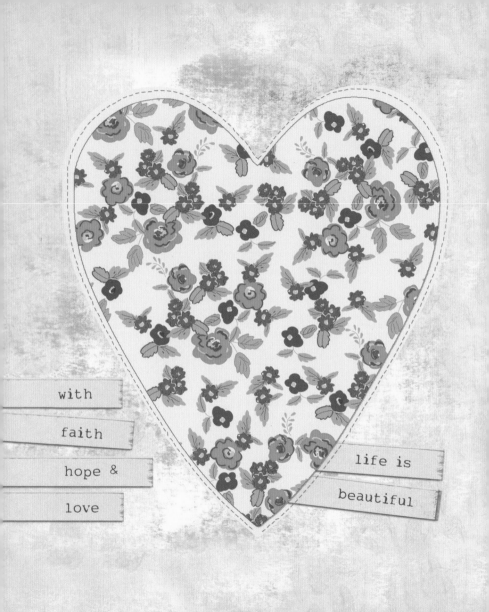

with

faith

hope &

love

life is

beautiful

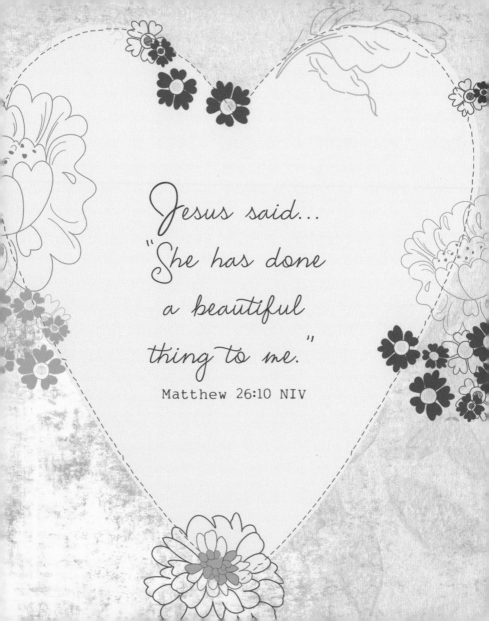

Jesus said...
"She has done
a beautiful
thing to me."

Matthew 26:10 NIV

Source of Pride

For I am not ashamed of the gospel of Christ, for it is the power of God to salvation for everyone who believes, for the Jew first and also for the Greek.

ROMANS 1:16 NKJV

What makes you proud? Is it your kids, and how they shine at school or their sports? Is it your job that you worked so hard to get? Your spouse? Your achievements? Your house, your car?

Jesus?

Gulp. Somehow, faith doesn't often factor into the "pride" equation because, for one, you have learned that it is sinful. Which can be true. Unless it is rooted in Jesus. Out of all the areas in life where you could place your pride, Jesus alone merits your boasts.

But the other problem lies in the godless climate around you. In today's culture, Jesus isn't politically correct anymore. Self-proclaimed tolerant and open-minded critics complain that His truth is too restrictive, and His ways are too narrow. Their voices are so loud that even well-meaning Christians cower in fear. No one wants to step on toes. Rock the boat. Or give them any more reason to hate or ostracize Christians.

Believer, it's time for you to boast. Not about who you are or what you've done, but about the gospel of Jesus Christ. You hold the antidote for eternal death, and you have no need to be ashamed. Praise God, instead, for the power you possess—the power to bring life to a dying world.

Like supernatural effervescence, praise will sometimes bubble up from the joy of simply knowing Christ. Praise like that is... delight. Pure pleasure! But praise can also be supernatural determination. A decisive action. Praise like that is... quiet resolve. Fixed devotion. Strength of spirit.

JONI EARECKSON TADA

May I never boast about anything except the cross of our Lord Jesus Christ.

GALATIANS 6:14 NLT

Reclined Dining

*The LORD answered Moses, "Is the LORD's arm too short? Now you
will see whether or not what I say will come true for you."*

NUMBERS 11:23 NIV

"What are we having for dinner?" your kids want to know.
They ask every day, usually right after eating their lunch. It
seems that from birth, people just want to know what's coming,
particularly when it comes to having their needs met.

The Israelites were no different. They were led out of
slavery in Egypt by a man they barely remembered and a God
they hardly knew. To make matters even harder, God led them
to a wilderness where food and water were hard to find. So they
did what people often do. They panicked. And complained.
They wanted to go back to being slaves again.

Little did they know what wonderful plans God had in
store. And with tremendous patience, God showed them. Day
by day, He provided manna, a special bread straight from
heaven. Quail flocked to their camps as their meat supply. And

water gushed from the most unlikely places, just so God could prove Himself sufficient for their needs. In the end, He led them to the Promised Land.

Do you harbor any fears about the future? Are you worried that God won't be able to take care of you, your job, your family, or that difficult circumstance that has been consuming your thoughts lately? Though panic and self-preservation may feel more familiar—like Egypt to the Israelites—don't head back into slavery. Release yourself into God's available rest. Marvel at His miraculous ability to meet your every need. Like manna from heaven, gather from His plentiful storehouse of grace and mercy in every moment of need.

Knowing God is putting your trust in Him. Trust that He loves you and will provide for your every need.

TOM RICHARDS

He rained down manna
for them to eat;
he gave them bread
from heaven.

PSALM 78:24 NLT

Rock the Boat

Peter got down out of the boat, walked on the water and came toward Jesus. But when he saw the wind, he was afraid and, beginning to sink, cried out, "Lord, save me!"
MATTHEW 14:29–30 NIV

You have to love Peter's heart. In the middle of the roaring wind and crashing waves, he spied Jesus walking on the water, and more than anything, Peter wanted to be with Jesus. So he stripped down and stepped out of the boat, right onto the water. For a moment, it was amazing!

But then his focus shifted. *Wait a minute. I'm standing on a lake with a scary storm swirling all around me*, Peter suddenly realized. His eyes looked down. His feet started to sink. *I can't do this!* he panicked. And he was right, he couldn't. But Jesus could. So Jesus caught him, lifting him to immediate safety.

It is a lot of fun to talk about God and His goodness. To stay comfortable keeping Christianity in the realm of discussion and theory. But God wants to meet with you in the heart of reality, to let you know He actually exists, controls each of your moments, and wants you to learn to trust Him in each one. Even if those moments look like giant waves about to drown you. Waves like bankruptcy, rebellious children, cheating spouses, failing health, or a frustrating job. Maybe you fear the future, or you hear God calling you to a task you don't want to do. The storms of life threaten to overtake you.

No matter how high the surf gets, keep your eyes firmly fixed on Jesus who not only can, but will save you. As you learn to trust, He will take your hand and steady your seasick legs. Then you can walk securely, peacefully, miraculously through whatever blows your way.

Jesus is in the boat with us, no matter how wild the storm is, and He is at peace. He commands us not to be afraid.

ELISABETH ELLIOT

Immediately Jesus reached out his hand and caught him.

MATTHEW 14:31 NIV

Reflections of Grandeur

When God created human beings, he made them to be like himself.
GENESIS 5:1 NLT

What would your ideal body be? What would you currently have to rearrange to achieve that image? If you're having trouble coming up with ideas, just check out the latest magazines lining the grocery store checkout. Or step into your local gym and marvel at the time, energy, and myriad of ways people work to shape or keep their body image. Image sculpting is a major phenomena in our culture.

You, however, were created to be more. Better than the most beautiful magazine model. More impressive than the biggest bodybuilder. You were made to bear the image of *God.*

When you look at yourself in the mirror, you see the reflection of someone whose unique make-up tells a much bigger story. You have a Creator who has formed you to think, love, speak, play, feel, see, smell, and taste, just like Him. There is no other creature on earth like you. No one who bears the beautiful imprint your unique soul brings to this world. You are an expression of God like no other, with an even greater glory yet to be revealed when you are fully perfected in Christ.

So the next time you notice how much more buff that other person's body is, remember your divine reflection. Revel in the truth that you are a unique image-bearer of Christ, and you wouldn't trade that look for anything in the world!

All that we have and are is one of the unique and never-to-be repeated ways God has chosen to express Himself in space and time.

BRENNAN MANNING

For now we see only a reflection
as in a mirror; then we shall
see face to face. Now I know in
part; then I shall know fully,
even as I am fully known.

1 CORINTHIANS 13:12 NIV

Oh, so delighted we're on this journey together.

Terri Conrad

Sweet Dreams

In vain you rise early and stay up late,
toiling for food to eat—
for he grants sleep to those he loves.

PSALM 127:2 NIV

Your alarm clock sounds, and another long day unfolds in your mind before your feet hit the floor. Considering the size of today's to-do list, you wonder how you're going to squeeze in time for a workout, not to mention time for friends, for family, for God.

So you start out with first things first. Pouring yourself a large cup of coffee, you curl up on the sofa and soak in the praise of Psalms, some wisdom from Proverbs, and a story from the gospels. Suddenly, the tyranny of the urgent starts losing its hold in light of God's imminent presence. You are known. Protected. Loved. Provided for. And the world's worries vanish as you enter the rest of your Father's care.

Now you are ready for the rest of the day. Not because you

are now fueled up to go do it on your own, but because you are filled with the knowledge of His presence as you go, and your spirit is at rest. You are assured that the God of glory you read about this morning will be just as glorious in your life today.

Child of God, do not stress. God invites you to rest—not only in your eternal future, but in every moment now, knowing He is sufficient for your every need today.

A quiet morning
with a loving God
puts the events of the
upcoming day into
proper perspective.

JANETTE OKE

In peace I will lie
down and sleep,
for you alone, LORD,
make me dwell in safety.

PSALM 4:8 NIV

Never Alone

*No one will be able to stand against you all the days
of your life....I will never leave you nor forsake you.*

JOSHUA 1:5 NIV

If you've ever experienced it as a child, you'll never forget
it: the moment you looked up from that toy that had so grabbed
your attention to find your family gone. Circling around, you
see they are nowhere in sight. You venture a few steps forward,
hoping to catch a glimpse, but strange faces are all you find.

You are alone, and panic sets in. What are you going to do?

As a kid, you're likely to burst into tears or beg someone
nearby to help you. Though it might seem like an eternity, it's
only a few moments until you and your loved ones reconnect.

But as an adult, what do you do when that sensation of
loneliness settles in your soul? The panic that comes when you
look up from life's busyness to discover the people who loved
you are gone. Maybe you've moved and are in a new place.
Your parents have gone to be with God. Or your friends have

just gone their own way. There's no intercom system or store clerk to bring them back to you.

Believer, no matter how lonely or isolated you feel, Jesus has promised to never leave you. It is impossible to look up and find Him missing. When you sit down, rise up, go to work, and sleep again, He is by your side. Lean into Him, and let your soul find satisfaction in His presence. He will be your faithful friend who quiets your panicked soul, takes your hand, and leads you to your Father.

We have been in God's thought from all eternity, and in His creative love, His attention never leaves us.

MICHAEL QUOIST

You have been with me from birth and have helped me constantly—no wonder I am always praising you!

PSALM 71:6 TLB

Ransomed

The Son of Man did not come to be served, but to
serve, and to give his life as a ransom for many.

MARK 10:45 NIV

You've seen it in the movies and occasionally in the news.
A victim has been taken hostage by kidnappers with an agenda:
they want as much money as they can get. Using the hostage's
life as bait, they wait until someone who cares enough will pay
the ransom.

If it happened to you, would anyone foot the bill? If so,
how high a price could they afford?

Whether you know it or not, you have been in this very
situation. A sinister enemy took you captive through your own
sin, holding you hostage under his tyrannical rule. The price on
your head? Higher than all the money in the world. It would
require a life for your life. But not just any life—the life of God,
Himself. God would have to agree to give up everything just to
get you back.

And He did. Jesus left the comfort of Heaven to live a perfect life that only He could live. Then He offered it up, paying your ransom, so you could be freed. So you would be His.

You, dear friend, are of infinite value to God. He proved it by sacrificing everything to buy you back. What more do you need to know? Enjoy your freedom, and live like you are loved.

We are of such value to God that He came to live among us...and to guide us home. He will go to any length to seek us, even to being lifted high upon the cross to draw us back to Himself.

CATHERINE OF SIENA

GOD paid a ransom to save you from the empty life you inherited from your ancestors. And the ransom he paid was not mere gold or silver. It was the precious blood of Christ, the sinless, spotless Lamb of GOD.

1 PETER 1:18-19 NLT

To Die For

If you live according to the flesh, you will die; but if by the
Spirit you put to death the misdeeds of the body, you will live.

ROMANS 8:13 NIV

The word is used so loosely these days. "I'd die to have a body like hers!" or "I'm dying to see what's going to happen." Maybe even, "I'd die before I'd let them do that to me!" Dying just seems to capture how passionately you feel about something, even if you really don't mean it to that degree.

God uses death to show His level of commitment, too. Only His words aren't for play. When God speaks, it's serious business. So when God told Adam that sin would result in death and separation, He certainly wasn't kidding. When He promised to send a Savior to solve that problem, He proved it through the death of His Son, Jesus. And when He raised Jesus from the dead and seated Him in heaven beside His throne, God spoke a final word over death: eternal life in Christ.

As God's child, you have been given victory over spiritual

death through life in Christ. But God has a very unique way to bring the life of His Son into you: death. Death to yourself— not in your physical being, but in the areas of your mind and heart that want to live on your own without Him.

Are you passionate about the God who gave His life for you? Then show it like He does. Die to the sinful desires that want to rule you, and submit to the new life of love and eternal hope in His Son. In this way, you're dying to live—for Jesus.

Dying for something is easy because it is associated with glory. Living for something is the hard thing. Living for something extends beyond fashion, glory, or recognition. We live for what we believe.

DONALD MILLER

Unless a kernel of wheat falls to the ground and dies, it remains only a single seed. But if it dies, it produces many seeds.

JOHN 12:24 NIV

The Loved Disciple

I pray that you, being rooted and established in love, may have power...
to grasp how wide and long and high and deep is the love of Christ.

EPHESIANS 3:17–18 NIV

Jesus chose twelve disciples. He lived among them and trained them all to see God and walk in His ways. Yet in the book of John, one of them seems to stand apart. He is identified as the disciple whom Jesus loved. This special person leaned against Jesus' chest at the Lord's supper. He received Mary as his own mother at Jesus' instruction from the cross. He witnessed the tomb, and the risen Lord on the shore. Each time he is mentioned, the reader is reminded, *this is the disciple Jesus loved.*

But wait a minute. Didn't Jesus love all his disciples? What is going on here?

John, the author of this gospel, recognized the amazing truth that God wants all of His kids to know. He wasn't just one of the masses. John had been singled out for Jesus' affection. Recounting the story of Jesus, he cast himself in that beautiful light.

When you think of yourself, do you feel the gaze of your Father's love? Like John, do you identify yourself as the disciple that Jesus loves? It may seem too good to be true. But God says it is. You are the disciple whom He loves. You are invited to recline on His chest, to witness His work, and to marvel at His miracles. You never have to feel lost in the crowd, unimportant, or unworthy. Jesus has called you to Himself so that, like John, you will see yourself in the beautiful, ever-glowing light of God's love.

Love is there for us, love so great that it does not turn its face away from us. That Love is Jesus. We can dare to hope and believe again.

GLORIA GAITHER

Jesus knew that the time had come to leave this world...Having loved his dear companions, he continued to love them right to the end.

JOHN 13:1 MSG

Love Waits

When Jacob saw Rachel, daughter of his uncle Laban,
and Laban's sheep, he went over...and watered his uncle's
sheep. Then Jacob kissed Rachel and began to weep aloud.

GENESIS 29:10–11 NIV

One look at Rachel and Jacob was smitten. He even
kissed her. He was going to make her his. Only there was one
problem. Rachel's dad wasn't ready to hand her over. Jacob
had to work to win her hand...for seven long years. Surprisingly,
Jacob didn't seem to mind. The time flew by since Jacob loved
her so much. To him, she was so worth the wait.

And that's how real love is. Love waits. Like Jacob, Jesus
waits for His beloved bride—you! He is at work even now,
preparing a place for you to be with Him. His Spirit inside you
works to make your heart like His. Life and love are in process,
waiting for that final moment when all will be made right, when
His love is completed in you.

Are you waiting patiently for Him as He is for you? Are you resting securely in His love, trusting that one day all the moments of your life will make sense as He promises they will? When the pressures and fears of this life light the fire of panic in your soul, put it out with Jesus' promise of love. Don't run ahead, trying to work out problems in your own power. Wait for God who alone can rescue you, who holds your future in the palm of His hands. Rest in His goodness. His plans to prosper you are so worth the wait!

So wait before the Lord.
Wait in the stillness.
And in that stillness,
assurance will come to you.

AMY CARMICHAEL

The LORD longs to be gracious to you; therefore he will rise up to show you compassion. For the LORD is a God of justice. Blessed are all who wait for him!

ISAIAH 30:18 NIV

Comforting Thought

God is our merciful Father and the source of all comfort. He comforts us
in all our troubles so that we can comfort others. When they are troubled,
we will be able to give them the same comfort God has given us.

2 CORINTHIANS 1:3–4 NLT

Your teenager is acting up, driving you crazy. You're
beside yourself and don't know what to do. You need to talk to
somebody, but who? Are you going to call that friend whose life
and kids seem perfect, or would you rather have someone who
can relate to how you feel?

When it comes to trials, you want help from people who
understand. Who won't judge or give cliché answers, but who
have wrestled in the same arena you now find yourself. Who
can lend you some of the wisdom they gained in the process.

God knows how you think. It's why Jesus didn't stay in the
comfort of Heaven, but subjected himself to life on this pain-
filled planet. He endured sadness and suffering so He could
comfort you in yours, understanding your heart and leading you

through His wisdom to a better place of comfort and peace.

Trials are no fun, and life would definitely seem better without them. In fact, you might work hard to avoid them. But God, your Father who loves you, says they will come. More than that, you are to accept them with joy. How?

Just as suffering enabled Christ to relate to you, so your trial will help you understand how to comfort others. Instead of resisting or resenting the hardship, trust that God's eternal purpose is at work in you, crafting Christ's character into you. Let God's cover of love and grace enfold you, even as your experience enables you to wrap His warmth around others who need it, too.

When you are in the dark, listen, and God will give you a very precious message for someone else when you get into the light.

OSWALD CHAMBERS

Encourage one another and build each other up, just as in fact you are doing.

1 THESSALONIANS 5:11 NIV

Divine Dialogue

Your ears shall hear a word behind you, saying,
"This is the way, walk in it," when you turn to
the right or when you turn to the left.

ISAIAH 30:21 ESV

What do you love about your best friend? Of all the qualities that come to mind, wouldn't the way you connect top the list? Deep friendships are formed through true, real communication. Trusting one another. Knowing the other's heart and hopes.

How, then, would you rank your relationship with God? Are your conversations more like monologues, where you talk a lot about what you need? Or is it richer, where conversation flows both ways as you spend time together?

God loves to spend time with His kids. He wants to hear what's on your heart and help you where it hurts. But God also wants you to hear His heart. He has thoughts and plans and hopes for you. Secret counsel to divulge. And special revelations about who He is. However, you will only hear it when you are still and listen. He promises that if you seek Him with all your heart, you'll find Him. In fact, you'll actually start to hear Him. His still small voice—the one that loud and busy schedules drown out—whispers the truth of His love. He reminds you of His ways. And He leads you where He wants you to go, all the days of your life.

To hear God, you have to stop talking and doing to be still before Him. Seek Him in His Word. Wait patiently, and listen for Him to speak. Then move with confidence in the direction that He leads you, knowing your best friend is with you all the way.

Be still, and in the quiet moments, listen to the voice of your heavenly Father. His words can renew your spirit... No one knows you and your needs like He does.

JANET L. SMITH

Be still,
and know that
I am God.
PSALM 46:10 NIV

The Age of Grace

Even to your old age and gray hairs
I am he, I am he who will sustain you.
I have made you and I will carry you

ISAIAH 46:4 NIV

It happens to everyone at some point. You look in the mirror, as you do every morning, but suddenly you notice something different. Little wrinkles are lining the skin around your eyes. Looking up, you notice new strands of gray in your hair. Reality dawns: you are getting old.

Of course, you can fight it. A plethora of lotions, pills, and beauty procedures promise to stave off the inevitable for at least a few more years. But the mirror doesn't lie. It tells you that time is passing by. That your life story will indeed have an end. It's a sobering thought.

For the believer, though, every gray hair signals hope, not despair. Though your body is getting older, God is at work inside renewing your spirit day by day. Times will change, friends will come and go, and our bodies will run out of steam, but God stays the same, and He will never leave your side. He will never stop caring for the one He planned from before time began. He has carried you from eternity past into your very present, and He will carry you all the way home where a new, age-free, wrinkle-free, sin-free body will be given to you. Getting older now just means getting closer to the Lord and the day you can live perfectly in His presence forever.

Today, take time to thank God for gray hair, and yes, wrinkles, too. Let each one remind you of your Father's incredible faithfulness in your past, present, and future.

God is the one who enables us to savor the moment and grow older joyfully.

LUCI SWINDOLL

We do not lose heart. Though outwardly we are wasting away, yet inwardly we are being renewed day by day.

2 CORINTHIANS 4:16 NIV

See Me

She gave this name to the Lord who spoke to her:
"You are the God who sees me," for she said,
"I have now seen the One who sees me."

GENESIS 16:13 NIV

Hagar thought she was alone. Unwanted. Hopeless. Forsaken by her master, she cried into the desert air, waiting for her death.

Then God spoke. Words of hope—in the middle of the wilderness—came from His heart, and Hagar was forever touched. *You are the God who sees me*, she understood. Being known by God meant being saved.

Friend, the same God who saw Hagar in her place of despair sees you, too. When you pour out your heart in your secret place, He sees your hurt and carefully collects your tears. Not one will be wasted. The truth is, though God is all-powerful and sovereign, wise and all-knowing, He is also all-caring. The troubles that burden your heart hurt His, too.

He weeps when you weep, and rejoices in your joy. Even in death, God cherishes His loved ones and leads them home.

Friend, God sees you, right where you are. He knows your thoughts, your worries, and your needs. He is closer than you know. Cry out to Him with all your heart, and He will quiet you with His love. Known and treasured by God, you will be saved today and always.

> We can be assured of this:
> God, who knows all and
> sees all, will set all
> things straight in the end.
> Even better, He will dry
> every tear.

RICHARD J. FOSTER

You keep track of all my sorrows.
You have collected all my tears in your bottle.
You have recorded each one in your book.
PSALM 56:8 NLT

Seal of Approval

When you believed, you were marked in him with a seal, the promised
Holy Spirit, who is a deposit guaranteeing our inheritance.

EPHESIANS 1:13–14 NIV

Some stores require that you show a receipt before you
can leave. The clerks just want to see it to be sure your items
have been properly purchased. It's no big deal, really, because
people are used to various stamps of approval that declare an
item to be valid and authentic. Maybe it's the date on the milk.
The raised seal on your birth certificate. Or the FDA approval
on your medicine. People want to know in concrete terms that
what they possess is real, good, and theirs to keep.

God wants you to know that spiritual matters are no
different. Though a changed life cannot bear ink from a
stamp, it does bear the marks of the indwelling Spirit of God.
Whenever someone commits his or her life to Christ, something
amazing happens in the unseen, spiritual realm. God actually
places His Spirit inside them as a permanent seal signifying
the transaction. No matter what, you belong to Him. You have

been properly purchased, and His Spirit is the receipt. You no longer have to wonder if God will grow tired of you or if your list of sins will send Him back to the store for a refund. No, God has placed His seal on you so you can know for sure that you forever are His child. That same spirit who guarantees your future in Christ is at work even now, shaping you into His image.

Knowing you are saved and loved is not a nebulous issue. God bought you at a very high price. His Spirit is your permanent stamp of approval!

God's grace is alive and at work in us. It is not a one-time event but the ever-flowing power at work in us by the Holy Spirit.

MICHAEL NEALE

He has identified us as his own by placing the Holy Spirit in our hearts as the first installment that guarantees everything he has promised us.

2 CORINTHIANS 1:22 NLT

As the moon reflects the sun, you,
dear friend, can light up the world
as a mirror of God's goodness.
May His grace and mercy follow
you all the days of your life, and
brighten your life with His love
that outshines the sun.

JENNIFER GERELDS

If you have enjoyed this book
or it has touched your life in some way,
we would love to hear from you.

Please send your comments to:
Hallmark Book Feedback
P.O. Box 419034
Mail Drop 100
Kansas City, MO 64141

Or e-mail us at:
booknotes@hallmark.com